PRAISE FOR BLAKE MIDDLETON

In *An Actual Person in a Concrete Historical Situation*, Blake Middleton has funneled the ghost of David Markson through his peculiar, dry, witty lens. These are wondrous messages you might find on any street, messages from a reliable witness to our slow civilizational collapse.

— MARCUS PACTOR, AUTHOR OF *BEGAT WHO BEGAT WHO BEGAT*

A brief examination of hopelessness that doesn't wallow in hopelessness, that celebrates things in spite of their decay or futility. Middleton confronts the unique futility of poetry with a unique poetry of futility.

— ZAC SMITH, AUTHOR OF *50 BARN POEMS* AND *EVERYTHING IS TOTALLY FINE*

I wish everyone would write like this—direct, detached, and with unbridled purpose.

— ANDREW WEATHERHEAD, AUTHOR OF *$50,000*

Thank god for writers like Blake Middleton, who can transform life's unrelenting ennui into a really compelling, funny, enlightening, and occasionally downright heart-warming book. This book is a reminder that you exist, but beyond that, it will make you feel human again.

— BENJAMIN DEVOS, AUTHOR OF *THE BAR IS LOW*

T0145764

AN ACTUAL PERSON IN A CONCRETE HISTORICAL SITUATION

BLAKE MIDDLETON

CL◢SH

For Grant

AN ACTUAL PERSON IN A CONCRETE HISTORICAL SITUATION

my coworker shows up to work with a five foot whaling knife and no
  one questions why

i walk forty-one floors on a stairmaster overlooking a river

at the grocery store a woman mumbles *my life is over* while staring at
  bagels

i sit in my car and eat a sandwich

insert three dollars into the wrong washing machine

stare at my stomach in the mirror again

the scenes of our lives resemble pictures in rough mosaic

time shrinks, expands, collapses

i flounder through an afternoon

embrace lightness for a weekend

it's 4 a.m., the sky is orange

the 6th largest pyramid in the world is a bass pro shops

i eat mushrooms and escape history

eager to force some life into words again

sitting in the living room of my small apartment

feeling lost and unsure of myself

been referring to my chihuahuas as *hogs* lately

at 23 i drank beer in a closet-sized bedroom and read sartre after
 twelve hour shifts

watched the sunrise and felt an immense hope for the future

i put a quarter in my shoe to feel anchored to the earth

a banana duct taped to a wall was sold for more money than i make in four years

i shouldn't be thinking about things like that

time makes the perfectly tolerable totally not

at work i'm a shitty actor playing a hungover waiter

i sit outside the coffee shop on a nice day

it's a normal thing to do—it feels good

i buy my homeless friend a pack of cigarettes, a gatorade, and a few
scratch-offs for christmas

i learn things then forget them

so what's the point

i walk to the river, sit on a bench, and admire dolphins

there isn't a right way to live, but there are plenty of wrong ways on mondays i play tennis

sports announcer on a youtube video i'm watching describes federer
   as a mongoose on amphetamines

my homeless friend nearly slits my throat while showing off his new
   box-cutter

questions raised in the course of a life are often disquieting,
   unanswerable

water sloshes in the gutters

we navigate through time with money

words create problems they can't solve

a three-legged dog wears a shirt that says *the guacamole is extra and so
   am i*

in iraq protesters stand outside the u.s. embassy and chant *death to
   america*

forgot what i was rebelling against

gonna read a five volume history of the french revolution instead of
looking for a job

what am i doing

i'm a paranoid alcoholic some beautiful mornings

i lie in the sun and laugh at my bank account

my neighbor brings me three peacock feathers and a bag of kratom to
thank me for the time i drove him to the hospital after he got
drunk and fell down twelve stairs

guy at the gym lifting fifty pound weights has a fifty pound weight
tattooed on his bicep

i mumble *fuck you* to a pile of trash i am trying to sweep up as my
co-worker walks past me, and have to explain that i'm not saying
fuck you to him, i am just talking to a pile of trash

i briefly convince jenna that mike pence has a tail

a functionally extinct marsupial is trending on twitter

i want a wine-lined bunker deep underground

i am useless and immature, but i like my small joys

absurdities are comforting

herring fish communicate with farts

when the founder of pringles died he was cremated and dumped into an empty pringles can

i squirm intuitively through life, laughing at the world

a man running a marathon crosses the finish line and says, *i pledge allegiance to the american dream*, and takes a shot of vodka

how do i navigate this world

what is the correct way to navigate an economy of bullshit

relationships grounded in mutual alienation—yes

walt whitman would have loved adderall

i feel like kim jung-un—i wanna get wildly drunk with dennis rodman

where can i buy a pair of concrete cowboy boots

how do i convert a pontoon boat into a functional road vehicle

is my chihuahua farting on my head intentionally

history is endless

nuance is nauseating

we know ourselves objectively as objects extended in time and space

we know ourselves subjectively—our private, small, self- consuming passions

[something subtle and inexplicable]

the culmination of world history gave us the four-loko fleshlight

i stop playing tennis on mondays

a condom advertisement tells me that i live on a big sexy world

the universe has no purpose

the motion of the solar system proceeds according to immutable laws

a man in an american flag onesie drunkenly climbs into a massive
   truck covered in aggressive bumper stickers

i'm tired of living in the united states of america

i'm tired of living in the space between what i am moved to do and
   what i can do

i'm an actual person in a concrete historical situation

infinitely confounded by the vastness of an already

immediately overwhelming world

i'm experiencing a world-weariness more characteristic of middle-age

i feel like ray romano

we admire gentle irony in our poets

but i'm tired of irony

i'm hungover at work, thinking about income inequality

only capable of caring about money when i don't have any

i drink wine to stop thinking about money and other things

i'm fucked in the head and my poetry sucks

successfully linking a succession of life situations seems impossible

i read biographies looking for ways to live

my head is full of hegel quotes—help

everything is unraveling significantly faster than most scientific
    models had predicted

thousands of migrants drown off the coasts of europe

a million species of animals and plants are at risk of extinction

carbon dioxide in the atmosphere has dramatically surpassed safe
    levels

it feels like the world is ending, but in a really slow and stupid way

but everyone knows the future is going to suck

we remind ourselves over and over and over again

the world is ugly and people are sad

but i still feel calm in nice weather

and you still have time to fall in love

i'm gonna spend twenty dollars on scratch-offs

the song of the infinite is compromised by the finitude of its terms

plagiarism is good

i'm an under 40 victim of fate

made myself dizzy jogging around a 0.071428571428571 mile track

i feel mildly autistic most days

william carlos williams is a stupid fucking name

i save up money

take an airplane to paris with the love of my life

at stollys i order us dark and stormy daniels and tip outrageously

meet a man wearing a jacksonville jaguars hawaiian shirt

he's from ireland

living as a tour guide in the latin quarter

we walk along the seine, he walks backwards, reciting facts

we take shots of flavored vodka in an american bar and chug
budweisers from the czech republic

we follow him into the basement of a scottish pub and listen to him
play the ukulele

smoke cigarettes in tiny room with a skinny chimney

listen to two french people argue about who is the most french

i buy roses from a hobo and hand them to jenna

it feels like a memory, movie-like and vivid

back in florida i'm the same person but with more intimate knowledge
    of places i'd rather be

the weather changes, i have money again

we take a cheap flight to mexico

drink jalapeño mezcal mixed drinks naked in a rooftop pool

swim through bat cave cenotes

a lot of people try to sell me cocaine

in new york kanye cuts his set short because kim got robbed

we're herded out by police wielding automatic weapons

my friend jacob falls down stairs

a stranger describes it as a mangling

we walk to a burger king in chinatown and jacob leans against a
    dumpster and chugs ranch dressing

the uber is on adderall, we suspect, driving 100 down the highway

we put jacob to bed and drink until sunrise

two years later we read on a rooftop in bushwick then drink
    presidentes at the narrows

i introduce ben to fernet, he makes a funny face, gifts me his last
    chicken finger

i talk drunkenly with theo about literary influences

peter gives me a copy of *milk & henny*

i read it out loud on the subway back to bed-stuy

i'm sitting in the living room of my small apartment

i'm sitting on the balcony of my medium-sized apartment

time behaves in elastic, elusive ways

200 square feet and a pool improves my worldview

i share an apple with my chihuahuas

i don't know what i think

don't even remember things i have thought

the best thing i learned from nietzsche was basically a fitness tip

a profound love of life incites a certain type of sadness

the failure of words to mirror the world gives me a migraine

should probably go to the gym and punch a bag

what should i think about

siri keeps lying to me about the weather

i had ambition once, now i'm just confused

i feel like dustin hoffman in the graduate, that scene where he's
    underwater in the scuba suit

i see a homeless man's asshole, the government gives me a thousand
    dollar gift card

i know what's wrong with the world and i know how to fix it

just kidding

but i know how to drink two bottles of wine

i know how to show up to work on time and never call out

i know that if you do a shitty job at work, but also show up on time
    and never call out, it makes it harder to get fired, and since you
    need money if you want to live in an apartment and eat food,
    it's good not to get fired from work

i almost never get fired from work

uncertainty, incompleteness, vastness

language is a form our curiosity takes

there has to be a meaning somewhere

a premonition of an unknown, vaster world

the gap between what we actually know and what we just think
   we know

words are restless

there is no closure, it doesn't stop

everything i think and do is boring

why should this be any different

i abandon the stairmaster for the rowing machine

i abandon the rowing machine

i hate the voice people use when they read poetry out loud

another hurricane season worse than the previous hurricane season

the things of the world are illusory—they shift and disappear
   constantly

'i fear that i am becoming an insane pervert' was my favorite line from
   a green light

i lost *$50,000*

einstein intuited the laws of the universe

therefore...

any jackass can write a poem

writing a good poem is infinitely easier than intuiting the laws of the universe

nothing feels urgent enough

i relax by the pool

jesus christ was born in 3 b.c.

life should reveal itself as an increasingly moving series of
    recognitions

the world is a shithouse

i wanna scream *shithouse!*

my friends keep overdosing

my allergies clear up—i confuse it for elation

i miss the way i used to think about the world

can't even get stoned and enjoy nature documentaries anymore i know that i know things, but it feels like i don't know anything

a tiny computer tells me what i want to say

life is so good

life isn't too damn bad

life is a little bit too much

life is a little bit of fun

life isn't good

life is so fun

life is so much better today

life is a bit of a little too much

life is so much more than a little fun

life isn't a bad idea

life is so much worse than i thought

life is so much better than i thought

ACKNOWLEDGMENTS

Thank you Jenna, Mom, Dad, Saige, Alex, Slime, Zach, and Kenny for everything. I love you all very much.

Thank you to Benjamin DeVos, Giacomo Pope, Leza Cantoral, Christoph Paul, and the nice people at X-R-A-Y for believing in and publishing my writing over the years.

Thank you to Marcus Pactor for teaching me everything I know. Thank you to Zac Smith and Andrew Weatherhead for the helpful edits/blurbs.

Blake Middleton lives in Florida.
He wrote *College Novel* (Apocalypse Party) and this book.

He tweets @dough_mahoney

WE PUT THE LIT IN LITERARY

CLASHBOOKS.COM

FOLLOW US

TWITTER

IG
FB

@clashbooks

Email
clashmediabooks@gmail.com